Pet Expert

DOGS

By Gemma Barder

WAYLAND

www.waylandbooks.co.uk

PET EXPERT: DOGS!

Dogs are great! They are the world's most-popular pet and it's easy to see why. Dogs are loving and loyal, but they also need lots of care and attention. In this book you'll learn everything you need to know about looking after your dog, setting up the perfect home for them, and the best way to keep them happy and healthy. You'll also find out how dogs became such compatible companions, as well as some pretty incredible canine facts along the way. In fact, why don't we get started right away?

CONTENTS

ANIMAL BABIES

DOS AND DON'TS

DOGGY DATA

DREAM HOME

DOGS, DOGS, DOGS!

Although there's a dizzying number of dog breeds, they are divided into six groups according to their relationship with humans over time. Here they are:

TERRIER

There are lots of different Terrier breeds and they are all confident, energetic, highly intelligent dogs – which makes them great family pets. Their name comes from the Latin *terra*, meaning 'earth', as Terriers were originally used to hunt small burrowing prey, such as rabbits, rats and mice.

MINIATURE SCHNAUZER

This neat little dog is a mix of a standard Schnauzer, Poodle and Affenpinscher.

AIREDALE

These brave little dogs were the first police dogs in the UK and worked with British soldiers in the First World War (1914-18).

JACK RUSSELL

This breed gets its name from the Reverend John Russell, who first bred them.

WORKING

A working dog is any breed that was traditionally bred to perform a job. This could include herding sheep, pulling a sledge, hunting large prey or rescuing people.

BORDER COLLIE

These sheep-herding dogs are said to be the most intelligent breed of dog.

HUSKY

These super strong dogs have a double coat of fur that keeps them warm in cold weather.

ST BERNARD

This iconic rescue dog is named after a dangerous spot in the Swiss Alps, called the Grand St Bernard Pass.

TOY

Toy dogs evolved from lapdog breeds (dogs that fitted nicely into the lap to be stroked and cuddled) as well as common breeds that have been bred to be smaller, such as the Miniature Poodle.

SHIH TZU

This famously adorable breed dates back at least 1,000 years and it comes from Tibet.

CHIHUAHUA

This pint-sized pup is the smallest dog breed in the world.

MALTESE

This well-mannered breed is thought to be the oldest European Toy dog breed.

THE OTHER DOG GROUPS INCLUDE:

GUNDOG: This group was trained to run to pick up any prey their owner had shot down. Golden Retriever, Cocker Spaniel, Poodle

PASTORAL: These dogs were bred to help look after, herd or guard livestock, such as chickens, pigs, cows and sheep. Bearded Collie, Corgi, Old English Sheepdog.

HOU ID

Like Terriers, Hounds are hunting dogs. They have an incredible sense of smell, often long droopy ears, and they are strong and capable. This group also contains some of the oldest known breeds of dog still around today.

DACHSHUND

This breed's long, flexible body makes it perfect for wriggling into burrows after small animals!

WHIPPET

These friendly dogs are very quiet – so they might not make the best guard dogs! Some Whippets don't bark at all.

BASSET

Its floppy ears aren't just for show! They flap smells up from the ground, making this breed a super-sniffing tracker.

UNCOMMON DOGS

Dogs are everywhere, right? But there are actually some breeds of dog that are so rare, there are only a few hundred left. With powerful noses and tuneful barks, these dogs are pretty special.

DID YOU KNOW?

The Neapolitan Mastiff is one of the rarest breeds in the world, and it's also a movie star! One of these lucky dogs starred alongside Daniel Radcliffe and Emma Watson as 'Fang' in the *Harry Potter* films.

OTTERHOUND

This breed comes from Britain and has a playful personality. Otterhounds were originally bred to hunt, but are now mainly show dogs and family pets. Despite their sweet nature, there are only 600 registered Otterhounds in the world.

Otterhounds are an ancient breed and have been around since the 1600s!

Otterhounds have webbed feet, making them great swimmers!

NEW GUINEA SINGING DOG

This musical little pup really lives up to its name. The New Guinea Singing Dog has a unique way of howling that is much more tuneful than other dogs. Although not many of these dogs live as pets, some people believe there could be lots more living in the wild.

TELOMIAN

These dogs were first bred in the Malaysian jungle, in Southeast Asia, and they are still the only breed of Malaysian dog that can be found outside the country. Telomians were originally kept to get rid of mice and rats (just like cats) but they are now mainly family pets. Although they don't look that different to other dogs, they developed brilliant climbing skills as their original jungle owners lived in houses on stilts!

FACT FILE

The most endangered breeds in the world are actually wild dogs.

■ The Ethiopian Wolf is found in the highlands of Ethiopia, Africa. Fewer than 500 are alive today.

■ The endangered Mexican Gray Wolf is half the size of its North American cousin and it is thought that there are only 97 left.

■ Darwin's Fox is actually a small wolf the same size as an average cat. It is almost extinct in the wild.

50% **16%**

In 2015, 50 per cent more French Bulldogs' births were registered in the UK, while in 2013 Welsh Corgis' births declined by 16 per cent.

PUPPY PATTER

Dogs are great at communicating with their human buddies. Find out everything you need to know to understand what your puppy pal is trying to tell you!

FACT FILE

When you meet a new dog, there are a few things you should do to make a great first impression:

■ Ask the owner's permission before you say hello - some dogs can be shy or nervous.

■ Let the dog sniff your hand (sniffing in the doggy world is like shaking hands in the world of humans).

■ Speak softly and calmly to the dog.

TAIL

Dogs wag their tails when they are in a happy and playful mood. Your pup will usually wag its tail when it first sees you, or if you are playing together. Dogs put their tail between their legs when they are scared, sad, or even if they feel guilty about pinching food off the kitchen table!

BELLY

Your dog will show its belly when it wants to make friends with other dogs – or when it wants a tummy rub from you!

EARS

The position of a dog's ears can tell us a lot about how they are feeling. If they are pricked up, your dog is relaxed and happy. If they are slightly forward, your dog is alert. When their ears are back, your dog is unhappy or anxious, and when they are flattened down, this means your dog is afraid.

NOSE

Despite what you might think, a dry nose isn't always a sign that your pup is ill. It could be that they simply need a drink, or that they have just woken up from a nap.

TEETH

Pet dogs don't usually bare their teeth, so if they do something is probably wrong. Dogs bare their teeth when they are cross and upset – this could be because they are afraid of another dog, or angry at being in pain. Give your dog space to calm down.

LEGS

A dog who is scared or anxious will lower their front legs so that they are cowering down, or they might have one paw in the air, preparing to run if they need to. Happy dogs with have their legs straight or slightly bent – ready for play!

PUPPIES

These adorable little bundles need a lot of love and attention because they are no longer with their mother. Now, it's up to you to help them develop and grow!

PICKING A PUPPY

Picking the right puppy for your home is very important. Talk to your family about what type of dog would suit you best. Bigger dogs need more room and a big garden to play in, while long-haired breeds need plenty of brushing.

All puppies are cute when they are little, but they grow up fast!

BRINGING THEM HOME

Puppies can be quite nervous when they are taken to a new home. Make sure you have a comfy dog carrier to put them in and a warm blanket. If the journey home is long, make sure you have plenty of water and food for them, too.

Give your new puppy plenty of love and play with them every day to welcome them into your family.

CARING FOR YOUR PUPPY

While your new puppy settles into your home, remember to keep things calm and quiet. They'll be learning all about their new environment – and all about you, too! Talk to a vet about what vaccinations your puppy needs to keep them healthy.

9 weeks

5-6 pups

Female dogs are pregnant for nine weeks.

An average litter has five to six puppies.

CANINE CARE

It goes without saying that you want your dog to be the happiest it can be. Find out the best ways to care for your dog.

NEW BEST FRIEND

Dogs are social animals. In the wild, they live in packs. Left on their own they can be quite unhappy, so spend plenty of time with your dog. You could play in the garden, give them a good brush or just tell them about your day!

KEEPING CLEAN

A happy dog is a well-groomed dog. Grooming means making sure your dog is brushed and clean. Different breeds will need different amounts of grooming, so make sure you know what's right for your pet.

WALKIES!

One of the most important parts of looking after a dog is exercise. Dogs need to be walked at least once a day and some breeds need more exercise than others. Make sure you have a good lead, some dog treats and a poop-scoop with you.

DID YOU KNOW?

Clipping a dog's nails is tricky and is best done by a vet. You can also take your dog to a grooming parlour (a doggy hairdresser) to get their fur and nails trimmed.

Dogs need two bowls. One for a constant supply of fresh water and another for their daily meals.

FLEAS AND WORMS

Although it's not very nice to think about, fleas and worms are a common problem for dogs. The best way to help your pet is to give them monthly treatments to stop them from picking up fleas and worms. Your vet will be able to tell you the best type of treatment for your dog.

2 months

3 weeks

Dogs need their claws trimming every two months. Don't bathe any dog more than once every three weeks as it could irritate their skin.

FACT FILE

TRAINING DAY!

It's a good idea to teach your dog the following basic commands:

SIT

This is important when waiting to cross the road on walks.

STAY

When you don't want them to follow you.

COME

Vital for getting your dog to come back to you when they are off the lead.

FETCH

A fun throw and retrieve game to keep your dog happy and fit.

Give your dog lots of fuss and a little treat when they do something right!

THE CANINE CODE

There are lots of rules to follow when you own a dog, and it can get quite confusing! Follow these simple guidelines to become the perfect dog owner.

DO:

introduce your dog to other dogs to get them used to being around other animals. ✔

give your dog a short name – one or two syllables is best. And avoid names that sound like commands! ✔

pick up your dog's poo using a biodegradable bag, put it in the bin and wash your hands afterwards. ✔

give your dog plenty of toys to play with. They like to be kept active. ✔

check your dog's paws after they've been on a long walk. ✔

treat your dog like one of the family. Dogs love to be part of a pack! ✔

DON'T:

pull or tug a dog's tail.
It will hurt and confuse them.

leave their water bowl empty
or dirty. Dogs need fresh
water to keep them healthy.

force them to play with dogs
they aren't used to.

give your dog chocolate.
Chocolate is poisonous to dogs.

leave your dog alone for
long periods of time.

let them off their lead unless you
are In a large field or park
where this is allowed.

✔ FOOD FOR DOGS ✘

dry dog food	fish	chocolate	onions
wet dog food	apple	avocado	nuts
yoghurt	cheese	dried fruit	grapes

THE BEST BED

When you love your pet you want to give them the best home possible. Find out how to make a safe and cosy home for your dog.

SAFE AND SOUND

Making your house safe for a dog is a bit like baby-proofing. Look around the rooms your dog will call home to spot any dangers, such as wires they might chew on, blinds they could get tangled in or cleaning products they could mistake for treats or toys.

BEDTIME

A dog's bed is very important to them. It's not just the snuggle factor you need to think about, it's where you position their bed, too. Make sure your dog's bed is somewhere they can watch family life go by and feel as though they are part of the action.

THE GREAT OUTDOORS

Your pup should spend lots of time in the garden, so you will need to make it a fun and safe place to be. Check that there are no holes in the fence and that the garden gate is secure. Keep an eye out for any poo and clear it up straight away.

KEEP IT CLEAN

Keeping your dog's home clean and tidy is an important way to keep them healthy. Wash their bowls out once a day and wash their bedding once a week.

FACT FILE

Here are some dog beds to choose from:

NEST
A round, padded middle with soft edges that forms a cosy nest. Perfect for small to medium sized dogs.

CAVE
These beds have little hoods and are great for dogs that feel the cold, such as hairless breeds.

COT
Great for large dogs with lots of fur, they sit just off the ground so the fur doesn't get tangled.

MATTRESS
Looks just like a mattress for people! Perfect for large dogs who like to spread out.

DID YOU KNOW?
Dogs love toys! They help keep your dog occupied and relaxed, and stop them chewing other things, like the furniture!

WALKIES THROUGH TIME

Dogs have been our best friends for a very long time. Learn how our four-legged pals have travelled through history with us.

STATUS SYMBOL

As thousands of years passed, dogs became seen as symbols of wealth and power. Ancient Egyptian pharaohs, Chinese emperors and Roman nobility all had dogs as companions. Romans used dogs for hunting, and the strongest breeds were sent back to Italy to breed there, too.

38,000 BCE

3100 BCE

1200s-1400s

WOLF HEART

The first domesticated canines are thought to be wolves who followed human tribes around, looking for scraps of food. Some believe this could have started as early as 40,000 years ago! Over time, wolves started travelling with tribes and humans began training them.

POSH PETS

Nearly all aristocracy and senior clergy had pet dogs, which is why dogs often pop up in portraits of important people. Noblewomen preferred smaller dogs that they could rest on their laps, while noblemen liked powerful hunting dogs.

The Basenji is one of the most ancient breeds of dog in the world. It is said to resemble the dogs kept by ancient Egyptian pharaohs.

A HELPING PAW

In the 1950s, a study done by a psychologist called Boris M Levinson (1907–1984) showed how dogs could be used in therapy sessions. He found that people were more relaxed and able to talk when a dog was around to make them feel safe and happy.

1870s

1950s

2000s

VICTORIAN LOVE

By the Victorian era, most middle-class homes had a dog. In 1873, The Kennel Club began registering the breeding of pedigree dogs in the UK. Soon after, in 1881, the American Kennel Club was formed. Both hold dog shows, such as Crufts in the UK. Queen Victoria (1819 – 1901) entered six Pomeranians in the 1891 Crufts dog show.

DOGS TODAY

Dogs are still the most popular pet in the world (closely followed by cats!). They have continued to serve and help humans in many different ways, including rescuing people, herding cattle, guiding the blind, aiding the police and being loving companions, plus so many more!

DISTINGUISHED DOGS

Dogs have such great personalities, it's no wonder some become famous! Find out the fascinating stories behind some of the most well-known pooches.

TOTO

Toto is the scrappy little pup who joins Dorothy on her adventures in The Wizard of Oz. He has appeared in books, films and television series based on the world of Oz and has even had a book written from his perspective: Toto: The Dog-Gone Amazing Story of The Wizard of Oz.

DID YOU KNOW?

The first dog to play Lassie was actually a boy called Pal! He played the part for 11 years.

LASSIE

Some say Lassie first appeared as a character in a short story by Elizabeth Gaskell. Others believe she was based on a real dog who saved a sailor's life in the First World War. However, Lassie became known all over the world thanks to the 1940s film Lassie Come Home and the TV shows that followed.

CORGIS

Queen Elizabeth II (1926–) was first given a Welsh Corgi puppy on her 18th birthday and she went on to breed them for many years. Her last Corgi was called Willow and was the 14th generation of the queen's first ever pup. Queen Elizabeth has had more than 30 Corgis during her reign.

SCOOBY DOO!

Scooby is a Great Dane who helps his friends to solve spooky mysteries, as well as making time to eat Scooby snacks with his best friend, Shaggy. The first *Scooby Doo* cartoon was shown in 1969 and the dopey dog is still around today. There have been TV shows, films and even video games featuring Scooby and the gang.

$10,000

$125

Moose the dog was paid $10,000 per episode to star in the American TV series, *Frasier*. The little dog who played Toto in *The Wizard of Oz* was paid $125 a week (which was more than most actors got paid in 1939 when the film came out!).

TOP DOGS

Big, small, brave and ... unusual! All these dogs have something in common – they are all record breakers!

TALL AND SHORT

Gibson, a Great Dane just like this one, measures a massive 107 cm tall, while Milly the teeny Chihuahua is just 9.65 cm which is about the same height as a mobile phone!

This little Chihuahua is still much bigger than Milly!

SPACE DOG

Laika was a very special dog. In 1957 she became the first animal to orbit Earth. What the space scientists learned from her trip helped make it possible for humans to travel safely in space.

51 million

89.1 million

There are 51 million pet dogs in the UK.

There are 89.1 million pet dogs in the US.

Australian **Cattle Dogs**, like this one here, can live for a very long time!

OLDEST DOG

A hard-working Australian Cattle Dog named Bluey became the oldest ever dog in 1939, when he lived to 29.5 years. The average age of a dog is between 8–15 years, although some smaller breeds can live longer.

LONGEST TONGUE

Mochi the St Bernard is the lucky owner of the longest dog tongue in the world. It measures 18.58 cm and is so big it usually lolls out of his mouth. Despite his claim to fame, his owners think he is the cutest dog on the block.

Many St Bernards, like this one here, have long tongues!

DOGGY DATA

If you think you know everything about dogs, be prepared to be amazed. Memorise these five fab facts to impress your friends.

1 CANINE NOSES ARE UNIQUE

The print a dog's nose makes is one of a kind, just like human fingerprints.

2 TIRED PUPS HAVE PRIMAL INSTINCTS

Dogs curl up to sleep because of their wild dog past. Wolves curl up to keep warm and protect their vital organs.

3 DALMATIANS DON'T ALWAYS HAVE SPOTS

When Dalmatians are born they are almost always pure white. Their spots develop as they grow.

4 GREYHOUNDS ARE SUPER SPEEDY

They are the fastest breed of dog and can run at over 72 kilometres an hour.

5 LABRADORS ARE SO PUP-ULAR!

In fact, Labradors are the most registered breed of dog in the world. They make good pets for families with lots of energy and space for them to grow.

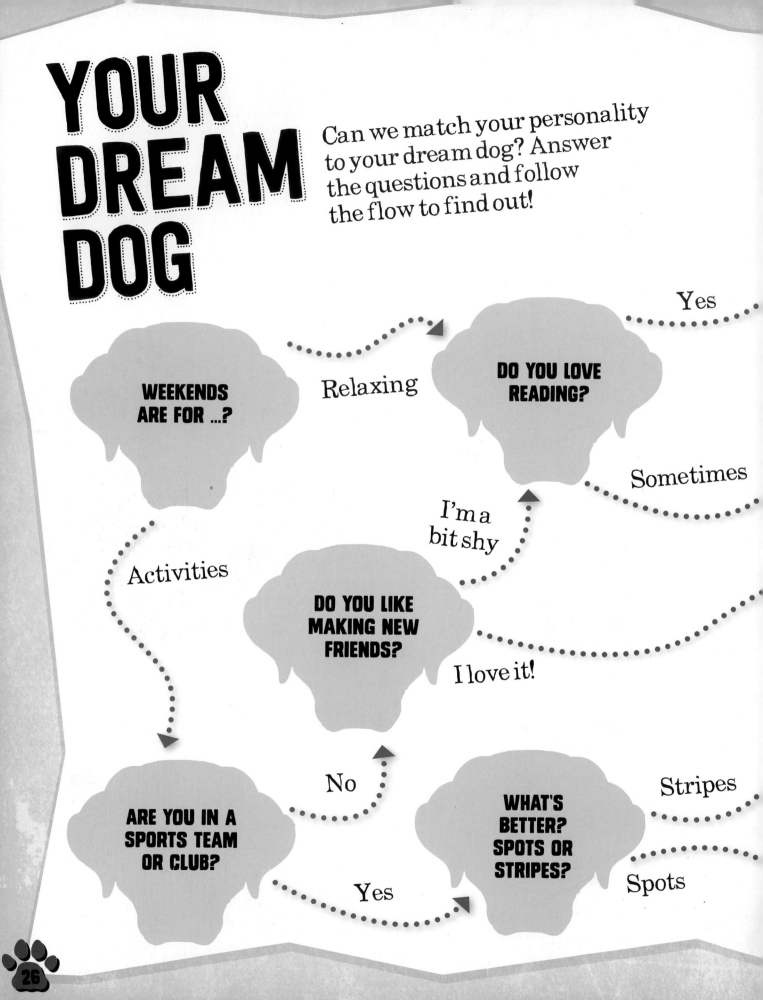

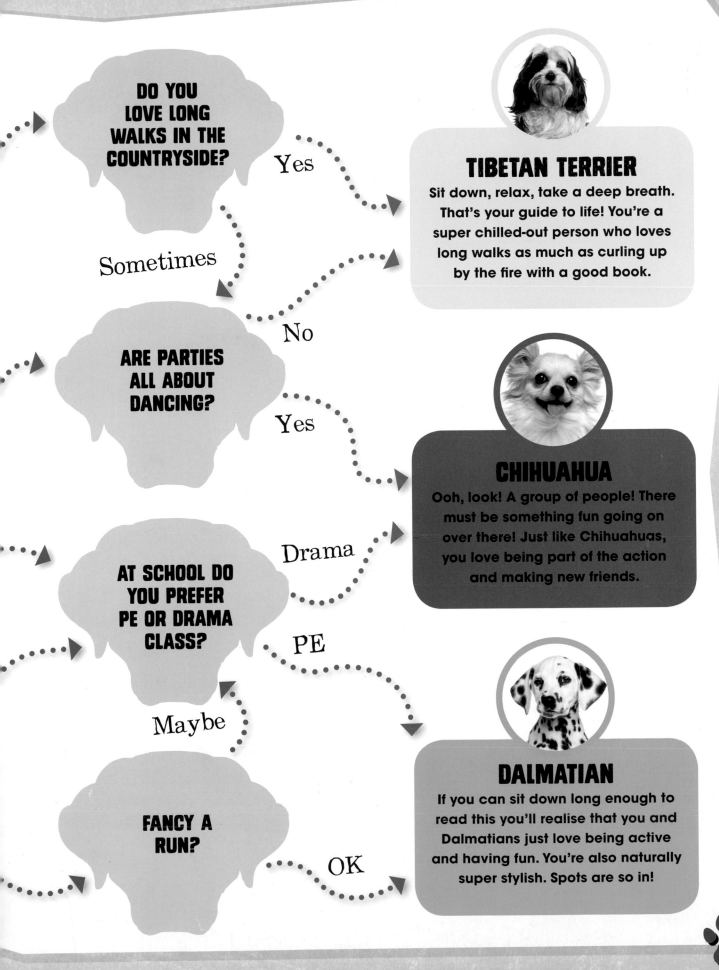

DO YOU LOVE LONG WALKS IN THE COUNTRYSIDE?

Yes

Sometimes

No

ARE PARTIES ALL ABOUT DANCING?

Yes

Drama

AT SCHOOL DO YOU PREFER PE OR DRAMA CLASS?

PE

Maybe

FANCY A RUN?

OK

TIBETAN TERRIER
Sit down, relax, take a deep breath. That's your guide to life! You're a super chilled-out person who loves long walks as much as curling up by the fire with a good book.

CHIHUAHUA
Ooh, look! A group of people! There must be something fun going on over there! Just like Chihuahuas, you love being part of the action and making new friends.

DALMATIAN
If you can sit down long enough to read this you'll realise that you and Dalmatians just love being active and having fun. You're also naturally super stylish. Spots are so in!

27

QUIZ!

Now let's put everything you have learnt in this book to the test! Yes, it's time to find out if you truly are a doggy expert.

1 WHERE DOES THE NAME 'TERRIER' COMES FROM?

a) the name of the person who started breeding them
b) the Latin name for 'earth' because Terriers like digging
c) the word 'terror' because they can be quite fierce

2 WHAT SHOULD YOU DO WHEN YOU SEE A DOG YOU DON'T KNOW?

a) ask the owner if you can stroke it
b) run over and stroke its back
c) throw it a ball

3 HOW LONG ARE DOGS PREGNANT FOR?

a) one month
b) nine weeks
c) six months

4 HOW OFTEN SHOULD YOU WALK YOUR DOG?

a) at least once a day
b) once a week
c) once every two weeks

5 WHICH OF THESE CAN BE POISONOUS TO DOGS?

a) chicken
b) rice
c) chocolate

The answers can be found on page 30.

6 WHAT TYPE OF BED IS PERFECT FOR HAIRLESS DOGS?

a) cave
b) mattress
c) cot

9 WHAT DOES A DALMATIAN'S COAT LOOK LIKE WHEN IT'S BORN?

a) white
b) spotty
c) hairless

7 WHAT TYPE OF DOG DID QUEEN VICTORIA ENTER INTO CRUFTS?

a) Welsh Corgi
b) Labrador
c) Pomeranian

10 WHICH OF THESE IS NOT A NEW BREED OF DOG?

a) Otterhound
b) Labradoodle
c) Cockerpoo

8 WHAT STORY FEATURES TOTO THE DOG?

a) Cinderella
b) The Wizard of Oz
c) Mary Poppins

GLOSSARY

BREED
A group of dogs who share a specific set of characteristics

CANINE
A Latin word that means 'dog', or anything relating to dogs

CARRIER
A plastic container big enough to transport your dog in. It's usually made out of plastic with lots of air holes and a handle for carrying smaller dogs.

DOMESTICATED
Animals that are living with humans as pets or working animals

ENDANGERED
At risk of extinction

GROOMING
Looking after your dog's appearance. This can include brushing, bathing and nail clipping.

HOUND
A hunting breed of dog

HUNT
To track down animals to capture or kill. Lots of dogs were originally bred and kept to hunt pests on farms.

KENNEL CLUB
An Organisation in the UK that oversees lots of doggy events and practices. They also have a list of registered breeders.

PUPPY
A young dog. Dog's stop being puppies at various ages depending on their breed

TERRIER
A small dog that was traditionally used to hunt out animals by burrowing in the earth

TOY
The name for very small breeds of dog

VACCINATION
Injections for puppies to prevent them from catching nasty canine diseases

VET
An animal doctor

WORKING
A collection of different breeds who have all been traditionally used for work

WAG
The tail of a dog moving swiftly from side to side

QUIZ ANSWERS

1. B.   2. A.   3. B.   4. A.   5. C.   6. A.   7. C.   8. B.   9. A.   10. A.

INDEX

First published in Great Britain in 2019 by Wayland
Copyright © Hodder and Stoughton, 2019
All rights reserved
Editor: Dynamo Limited
Designer: Dynamo Limited
ISBN: 978 1 5263 0859 7

Printed and bound in China
Wayland, an imprint of
Hachette Children's Group
Part of Hodder and Stoughton
Carmelite House
50 Victoria Embankment
London EC4Y 0DZ
An Hachette UK Company
www.hachette.co.uk
www.hachettechildrens.co.uk

MIX
Paper from
responsible sources
FSC® C104740

The website addresses (URLs) included in this book were valid at the time
of going to press. However, it is possible that contents or addresses may
have changed since the publication of this book. No responsibility for any
such changes can be accepted by either the author or the Publisher.

Picture acknowledgements:

**All images courtesy of Getty Images iStock
apart from: P1 Shutterstock, P7 tr Shutterstock,
P7 Westend61 GmbH/Alamy 7 cr
(Key: tr-top right, cr-centre right)**

Every attempt has been made to clear
copyright. Should there be any inadvertent
omission please apply to the publisher
for rectification.